SUMMARY OF THE CRUISE CONTROL DIET
BY JORGE CRUISE

Automate Your Diet and Conquer Weight Loss Forever

BY

DEPENDABLE PUBLISHING

COPYRIGHT

This publication is protected under the US Copyright Act of 1976 and other applicable international, federal, state, and local laws. All rights are reserved, including resale rights. You are not allowed to reproduce, transmit or sell this book in parts or in full without the written permission of the publisher. Printed in the USA. Copyright © 2019, Dependable Publishing.

DISCLAIMER

This book is a summary. It is meant to be a companion, not a replacement, to the main book. Please note that this summary is not authorized, licensed, approved, or endorsed by the author or publisher of the main book. The author of this summary is wholly responsible for the content of this summary and is not associated with the original author or publisher of the main book in any way. If you are looking to purchase a copy of the main book, please visit Amazon's website and search for **"The Cruise Control Diet: Automate Your Diet and Conquer Weight Loss Forever, by Jorge Cruise"**.

TABLE OF CONTENTS

CHAPTER 1: TIMING IS EVERYTHING 14

KEY TAKEAWAYS 14

1. The two main categories of diet plans are calorie-restrictive and food-restrictive diets. 14

2. Continuous eating triggers insulin production. 14

3. Insulin, not excess calories, makes you fat. 14

4. You can lower insulin level by paying attention to when you eat. 14

5. Avoid high-carb, low-fat, processed food. 14

SUMMARY 14

What Makes You Unhealthy and Fat 15

The Clock's Power 16

Fasting – The Ancient Secret of Health! 17

Understanding How Your Body Works 17

The History of Fasting 17

CHAPTER 2: TURNING ON CRUISE CONTROL AND STARTING TO BURN 19

KEY TAKEAWAYS 19

1. The Cruise Control program gives you the benefits of fasting without any side effects. 19

2. You can time and manipulate your nutrients. It is important to learn how to do this. 19

3. Take friendly fats and caffeine. They'll help you to lose weight easily. 19

4. A blood test is the most accurate method of testing for Ketosis. 19

5. Having lower ketosis helps burn more fat. 19

SUMMARY 19

Four Steps Involved in Turning on Cruise Control 20

    1. Nutrient Timing 20

    2. Nutrient Manipulation 21

    3. Fats that are Friendly 21

    4. Caffeine 21

Cruise Control Coffee 21

How to Prepare Cruise Control Coffee? 22

CHAPTER 3: GET A BOOST: EATING MATTERS, TOO 23

KEY TAKEAWAYS 23

1. Restrict your main meals to an eight-hour period 23

2. It is important to eat an anti-inflammatory diet 23

3. Not all fats are bad. 23

4. Avoid artificial sugar and processed foods. 23

5. Take in the right amount of protein..23

SUMMARY 23

The Benefits of Boost Zones..24

What Does It Mean to Eat Healthy on Cruise Control? 24

The Cruise Control Rules of Eating...24

Boosting Your Nutrition 25

Proteins..25

Fats 26

CHAPTER 4: MINDSET & MOTIVATION 27

KEY TAKEAWAYS 27

1. Cruise Control will help you achieve your desire only if you are devoted and tenacious...27

2. Your body needs fiber to remove excess waste. 27

3. Have a reason for embarking on the Cruise Control program. 27

4. Track your progress. 27

5. Give preference to yourself! 27

SUMMARY 27

The Key to Success Is Commitment..28

What to Expect..28

Have Goals...29

Strategies to Motivate and Win 29

Tips on Staying Motivated When Emotional Eating Calls............30

CHAPTER 5: YOUR FOUR-WEEK PLAN 31

KEY TAKEAWAYS 31

1. Commitment is needed in order to guarantee success............31

2. You can live your life without limitations while on Cruise Control. 31

3. Sleep is an important part of the burn zone. 31

4. Drink plenty of water. 31

5. Consume lots of vegetables. 31

SUMMARY 31

Choose Your Gear 32

Follow My Meal Planner 32

Choose foods that are approved by Cruise Control 32

Make Cruise Control Recipes..32

Mix and Match 32

Automate Your Schedule 33

Don't Change Your Life 33

Shop, Prepare, and Eat 34

CHAPTER 6: RECIPES................................... 35

BURN ZONE BREAKFAST BEVERAGE RECIPES........................35

Cruiser Coffee...35

Cinna's Coffee 35

Hot Cocoffee 36

Coconutty Coffee 37

Butter-Up Tea 37

BURN ZONE TREATS RECIPES 38

Either-Or Chocolatty Mousse 38

Buttery Goodry Icedrops 38

Vanichia Pudding 39

Strawberry Cream Pops 40

BOOST ZONE MEALS RECIPES 40

Either-Or Omelet 40

Good-Pot Shrimp Alfredo 41

Cruiser-Rave Portobello Mini-Pizza 42

Tunachia Salad 43

Turkey-in-a-Bento Box 43

Stir Fry in the Zone 44

BLT Ranch Wrap 45

Cashew Chicken Breast 45

Goat Cheese & Ham Frittata 46

BOOST ZONE SNACKS RECIPES 47

Golden Cheese & Cabbage Chips 47

Cheese & Broccoli Bread Rendezvous 48

Pepperoni Pizza Chips 48

Cream Cheese Celery Boat-load 49

Caulieese Muffins 49

The Cruiser Everything Bagel Topping (aka The Fierce) 50

BOOST ZONE DESSERTS RECIPES 51

Chocolatty Avo Pops 51

Choco "More!" Pudding 52

The Malibu Million-Dollar Handshake Milkshake 52

The Nutty Chocolatty Macadamit (!) Parfait 53

The Almond Butter-Up "Pacesetter" Cookies 54

Blessed Mug Cake 54

CHAPTER 7: THE EXERCISE EFFECT 56

KEY TAKEAWAYS 56

1. Aim for exercises that get your heart thumping. 56

2. Exercise improves your mood and physical health. 56

3. You should aim to exercise near the end of the burn zone, in the morning. 56

4. Muscle burns fat. 56

5. Burning melts fat faster. 56

SUMMARY 56

Learning to Exercise from Animals 57

Movement: A Medicine for the Mind 57

Short Bursts of Exercise Boosts Your Burn! 58

The role of catecholamine in boosting your burn 58

Principles behind the Cruise Control Workout 59

CHAPTER 8: YOUR CRUISE CONTROL WORKOUT 60

KEY TAKEAWAYS 60

1. Aim for 80% to 90% of your capable intensity during the high-intensity movement. 60

2. Moving between high intensity exercises speeds up lactic acid removal. 60

3. Focus on the quality of your moves, not just quantity. 60

4. Get enough rest. 60

5. Fuel your workout by rehydrating and getting enough electrolytes. 60

SUMMARY 60

High-Intensity Moves 61

Some High-Intensity Moves 61

The Role of the Low-Intensity Moves 62

Room for Flexibility 62

Warming Up and Cooling Down 63

How To "Engage" Your Core While Exercising 63

Reward Yourself After Each Week of Workouts. 64

Rest Day and Alternative Activities 64

Rejuvenating and Recovering After A Workout 64

Fueling Your Workout 65

CHAPTER 9: HEALTHY LIVING - ANYWHERE, ANYTIME 67

KEY TAKEAWAYS 67

1. Due to its high level of flexibility, Cruise Control is a fitness solution that is available for all persons. 67

2. Never go anywhere without your insulated water bottle. 67

3. Avoid sweeteners as much as possible. 67

4. Use Cruise Control-friendly sweeteners. 67

5. Be moderate in your use of alcohol. 67

SUMMARY 67

Nutrition 68

Eating Out on Cruise Control 69

Smart Food Shopping 70

Navigating Roadblocks 71

CHAPTER 10: YOU'VE GOT QUESTIONS, I'VE GOT ANSWERS 72

KEY TAKEAWAYS 72

1. You burn fat when you fast, not muscles. 72
2. It is possible to be a vegan on Cruise Control. 72
3. Close monitoring is needed for diabetics on Cruise Control. 72
4. You can take your usual vitamins and supplements during the Burn Zone. 72
5. There is no room for nutrient deficiency on Cruise Control. 72

SUMMARY 72

Won't My Body Slip into Starvation Mode When I Fast? 73

Will Fasting Burn Up My Muscle Tissue? 73

Will I Get Low Blood Sugar When I Fast? 73

Doesn't fasting slow down my metabolism? 74

Will I Become Nutrient-Deficient? 74

CRUISING FAQS 74

Can I Eat as Frequently as I Want During the Cruise Zone? 74

What about Coffee, Tea, Cream, Or Milk During the Burn Zone? 75

Isn't Breakfast the Key to Weight Loss? How Then Can Skipping It Be Healthy? 75

ONWARD! THE OPEN ROAD: WEEK FIVE AND BEYOND 76

KEY TAKEAWAYS 76

1. Now that you have arrived at your final destination, your next objective is to never quit, but to keep living all the lessons you have learnt from the Cruise Control program. 76

2. Cruise Control is not a diet or a fad or a temporary thingy. It is a lifestyle. 76

3. In order to consolidate your gains by continuing to live the Cruise Control lifestyle, you can let me be your online coach. Check out my Platinum Program at JorgeCruise.com. 76

4. Or you can let this book coach you by revisiting this book frequently and following the guidelines and menus all over again. 76

5. Or you can be your own coach. The required guidelines, tips, strategies, knowledge, food lists, meals, recipes, and meal planners, etc. have all been provided to you via this book. So just take over! Take control! Take charge! Coach yourself. You can do it! 77

6. Stay in touch with the Cruise Control program at JorgeCruise.com.; Facebook.com/JorgeCruise; and #CruiseControlDiet. 77

SUMMARY 77

YOUR CHOICES 77

1. Let Me Be Your Coach 78

2. Let the Book Coach You 78

3. Be Your Own Coach (BYOC) 78

APPENDIX A: THE GROUNDBREAKING SCIENCE BEHIND CRUISE CONTROL 80

KEY TAKEAWAYS 80

1. The pattern of eating on Cruise Control boosts your Mitochondria, which then improves your level of insulin sensitivity. 80

2. Cruise Control will help your body build needed antioxidants and burn free radicals. 80

3. Cruise Control directly burns belly fat. 80

4. The pattern of eating on Cruise Control will reduce your risk of heart disease, cancer, and diabetes. 80

5. Following the Cruise Control program will improve your memory, focus, and clarity. You will also reduce anxiety, stress, depression. 80

6. Cruise Control takes advantage of the regenerative and natural healing processes in your brain and body and ensures that you live better and longer (increases longevity). 81

SUMMARY 81

Power Up Your Mitochondria 81

Giving Adequate Time for Cleaning and Repairing 82

Burn Off Belly Fat Like You've Never Done Before 82

Become A Machine That Fights Diseases 82

Sharpen Your Mind 82

Live A Healthier, Longer Life! 83

NOTES 84

CHAPTER 1: TIMING IS EVERYTHING

KEY TAKEAWAYS

1. The two main categories of diet plans are calorie-restrictive and food-restrictive diets.

2. Continuous eating triggers insulin production.

3. Insulin, not excess calories, makes you fat.

4. You can lower insulin level by paying attention to when you eat.

5. Avoid high-carb, low-fat, processed food.

SUMMARY

There has been a lot of varying, misleading and sometimes conflicting suggestions regarding how to successfully lose weight. The simple truth, however, is that every diet plan can be divided into two basic groups: calorie-restrictive and food-restrictive diets. The calorie-restrictive diets are weight-loss strategies that focus on eating fewer calories than the body requires, while food-restrictive diets are weight-loss strategies that focuses on the type of food that should or should not be taken.

Insulin plays a major role in determining whether we will be fat or not. The main purpose that this unique hormone serves is to store fat in order to protect you from starving, but since food is readily available in our age, we are never in danger of starving – a concept your body does not seem to understand, this explains why we still produce insulin and store fat the way we do.

What Makes You Unhealthy and Fat

It is imperative to understand why you are fat in the first place; contrary to popularly-held belief, insulin is the hormone that makes you fat or obese, not excess calories. The main purpose of insulin is to store fat. This stored fat will serve as a reserve of energy when there is limited access to food. This phenomenon helped keep the early men alive. In modern time however, most of us get food whenever we want, so the importance of the fat-storage role of insulin has reduced. Yet your body does not seem to understand the difference and so keeps on producing insulin as if we are still early men.

A major job of insulin is to move glucose from your bloodstream into your cells where they will be stored as energy. Here is how it should work: when you eat something, the food increases your blood sugar, this increase sends a signal to your pancreas to produce and release insulin. Now, with insulin serving as the escort, your cells will allow the glucose to come on inside to be stored or used as energy. The problem we have today, regarding an epidemic of metabolic diseases (such as obesity and diabetes) is often as a result of our eating too often and too much. And the foods we often eat are those that spike insulin.

But there's good news. And the good news is that you can tell your body to stop the fat-storing anomaly.

The Clock's Power
So, to lose weight and to prevent or fight off many metabolic diseases, it is crucial to maintain the body's insulin level within normal range. The most effective way to lower your insulin level is to pay close attention to when you eat. Although, my diet pays attention to optimally combining fat, protein and carbs, but you must note that ***proper timing is the key to effortless weight loss!***

You see, your body runs on several timing systems known as circadian rhythm. And the truth is that you have clocks in virtually every cell in your body, with the clock in your brain being the master clock. These clocks tell you when to engage in specific activities such as sleeping, waking up, eating etc. The problem with the modern man is that his modern lifestyle and his internal clocks doesn't synchronize. Yes, what we lack is synchronicity!

Since we no longer flow with our default rhythm, our brains no longer know when to get sleepy or wakeup, and our stomachs no longer know when to be hungry and when to be satisfied.

Fasting – The Ancient Secret of Health!
When you eat less frequently, a message is sent to your body to produce less insulin. The logic here is to create long enough and recurrent enough periods of not eating such that will force your body to stop storing and instead start burning fat. The body actually thrives on fasting. This is because fasting lowers insulin and increases metabolism.

Understanding How Your Body Works
Your body's metabolism can be likened to an orchestra since it harmonizes a lot of metabolic processes. These processes can be largely categorized into two pathways: one transforms the food you eat into energy that can be stored or excreted, while the second breaks the molecules of stored energy down for your body to use as fuel. Like an orchestra, the body hates discord and chaos. What the body wants is absolute synchronicity. Some of the ways through which you can achieve such synchronicity are as follows:

- Charging up your calorie-burning engine
- Knowing what not to eat, and
- Understanding how eating the wrong foods can beat you down.

The History of Fasting
Fasting can be traced back to ancient civilizations such as the Greeks, who fasted on purpose as a strategy for cleansing, purifying, and detoxifying the

body. Also, three of history's most influential men – Jesus Christ, Buddha, and Muhammad all believed in the healing power of fasting.

You can practice the ancient technique of fasting with my modern spin. This modern spin will help you achieve all the benefits of fasting without the drawbacks.

CHAPTER 2: TURNING ON CRUISE CONTROL AND STARTING TO BURN

KEY TAKEAWAYS

1. The Cruise Control program gives you the benefits of fasting without any side effects.

2. You can time and manipulate your nutrients. It is important to learn how to do this.

3. Take friendly fats and caffeine. They'll help you to lose weight easily.

4. A blood test is the most accurate method of testing for Ketosis.

5. Having lower ketosis helps burn more fat.

SUMMARY

The Cruise Control has been of immense help to so many people by helping them to reap the various benefits of intermittent fasting while avoiding the adverse side effects. The benefits of intermittent fasting include the energizing of the brain and mood boosting. The Cruise Control program also increases the level of ketones in the body without you needing to abstain from carbs.

Without a doubt, ketogenic diets have been around for long now, but Cruise Control is actually new! You see, I have discovered a way for you to harness the benefits of ketosis without experiencing any of its downsides. Staying in ketosis for a long time can lead to low body temperature, adrenal fatigue, and even bad breath. You might also need to know that contrary to popular belief, ketosis is not only for men, and Cruise Control works perfectly for both men and women. A lot of Cruisers are already seeing the benefits of Cruise Control.

Four Steps Involved in Turning on Cruise Control

The Cruise control program is a pleasant blend of modern nutritional science and ancient dietary wisdom. Cruise control achieves complete body transformation with multifaceted approach. Strategies that you will be incorporating during the program will address physiological, psychological, sociological, and genetic components. Four secrets are involved in the Cruise Control program.

1. Nutrient Timing

This step deals with the consumption of food nutrients in sync with your body's boosting and burning cycles. By consuming solid foods within a specific window of time each day, your body is equipped to fully utilize the nutrients you eat.

2. Nutrient Manipulation

In the Cruise Control program, you will be able to manipulate your nutrients' intake at different times of the day. Doing this will help ignite your body's natural fat burning ability and boost your metabolism. This can be done by (1) eating a wide variety of foods that are rich in fats and oil (2) enjoying a moderate amount of high-quality protein (3) and enjoying a reasonable amount of healthy and nutritious carbohydrate-containing diets.

3. Fats that are Friendly

A form of saturated fatty acids that comes with a lot of health benefits is Medium-Chain Triglycerides (MCTs). A top source of MCT is coconut oil. As part of a healthy diet, ***coconut oil and MCTs can help raise the metabolic rates and increase satiety***.

4. Caffeine

A delicious recipe for Cruise Control coffee has been developed by me. The coffee is filled with energizing caffeine and antioxidants. Research indicates that a cup of coffee can increase ketones and also boost your mood

Cruise Control Coffee

The cruise control coffee is a high-performance beverage that has great impact on your cognitive function and energy level. I have seen Cruise Control Coffee help a lot of persons

How to Prepare Cruise Control Coffee?
1. Brew 1 cup of ground coffee with filtered water
2. Add 1 or 2 tablespoons of MCT or coconut oil. start with a tablespoon and slowly increase
3. Add 1 to 2 tablespoons of grass-fed, unsalted butter
4. Add a little Himalayan pink salt to energize the body with electrolytes
5. And mix with a spoon or blender until it looks like foamy latte

The benefits of the Cruise Control Coffee are: serenity and satisfaction, strong and stable energy, a sharp mind, metabolic boost, reduction in pain and inflammation, more intense workouts and metabolic boost.

CHAPTER 3: GET A BOOST: EATING MATTERS, TOO

KEY TAKEAWAYS

1. Restrict your main meals to an eight-hour period.

2. It is important to eat an anti-inflammatory diet.

3. Not all fats are bad.

4. Avoid artificial sugar and processed foods.

5. Take in the right amount of protein.

SUMMARY

You should take your main meal during an eight-hour window period (boost zone) that you decide on. Although you might decide to reduce this window period to about five or six hours. Research into time-restricted eating shows that an eight-hour window will provide you with all the fat burning, and effortless weight loss that you need.

The purpose of the boost zone time is to turn consumed food into high-octane fuel. You can always adjust your burn and boost zone to a time that is convenient for you. While what is optimal for me might be 10 A.M. to 6 P.M., 12 P.M. TO 8 A.M. might just do it for you. The most important thing here is that you restrict your main meals to a period of eight hours per day.

The Benefits of Boost Zones

There are a lot of benefits attached to boost zones. They include: a balanced hormone, no feeling of hunger, effortless weight loss, improved feeling of well-being and amplified happiness, strong and steady energy, healthy digestion, reduced inflammation and fortified immunity.

What Does It Mean to Eat Healthy on Cruise Control?

Relying on calorie counting or on macronutrient-based guideline is a complicated, cumbersome, and ineffective process. These are some of the pitfalls that Cruise Control avoids. And the whole idea of Cruise Control is pretty simple: there are two speeds – boost and burn, both of them are automatic. All that needs to be done by you is to focus on eating certain types of delicious meals in one zone, and take other decadent treats in the other zone.

I am not about self-inflicted suffering, rather, I am about effective and simple results. Cruise Control focuses on what s specific food does inside the body once it has been metabolized.

The Cruise Control Rules of Eating

The rules governing Cruise Control eating are:

(1) Eat unprocessed, whole foods.

(2) Avoid refined grains and sugars.

(3) Eat more of natural fats.

(4) Try as much as possible to eliminate artificial fats.

Boosting Your Nutrition

Now, the time has come to discuss how to qualitatively fuel up on Cruise Control in order to burn excess fat and harness the full potential of your body's metabolism. We will soon be discussing about the kinds of foods that will lower your blood sugar, increase your metabolic rate by 14 per cent, and increase your human growth hormone.

Proteins

Protein is made up of various chains of amino acids. Proteins exist in every cell of the body, and they create the building blocks that make us up. They build, repair, and maintain muscles, bone, cartilage, skin, and lots more. Where do the amino acids that produce protein come from? They are basically gotten from the food that you eat. Amino acids reconstruct inside the body to create unique configurations to make the shapes that makes the protein which eventually makes the human being.

Since dietary proteins are most demanding on your digestion when it comes to how they must be taken apart, you actually burn more calories when digesting proteins than any other nutrient. You should also note that getting enough of proteins is the way to keep the muscles from going to flabs. As you age, you will need more protein in order to prevent the loss of muscle.

Fats

I admit that it is hard for you to accept the idea that greasy and gelatinous fat is good, but this type of fat is actually different. Eating the fat on the Cruise Control meal plans is going to burn off the excess fat in your body! Healthy fats burn more cleanly and contain more energy than proteins or carbs. This is because fats don't have to be put through any form of metabolic assembly in order to be stored. Another reason is that a gram of fat provides almost twice as much energy as a gram of protein or carbohydrate.

CHAPTER 4: MINDSET & MOTIVATION

KEY TAKEAWAYS

1. Cruise Control will help you achieve your desire only if you are devoted and tenacious.

2. Your body needs fiber to remove excess waste.

3. Have a reason for embarking on the Cruise Control program.

4. Track your progress.

5. Give preference to yourself!

SUMMARY

Now that we have discussed the basics of Cruise Control, it's time to invest in your mind. Your mind responds to whatever you feed it. You need to have a few practical strategies that will give you the turbocharge that you need if you will be successful with Cruise Control.

You will be learning about tips on how to improve your chance of succeeding, check-ins and tracking, navigate mind blocks, engage in empowered self-talk, and set achievable goals. There are also some common mind blocks that will be reviewed, including everything you need in order to be revved up for a long, happy, and healthy life.

The Key to Success Is Commitment

Grit, tenacity and devotion are the factors on which your success depends. You need to set your own intention and motive, the truth is that no one will care about your health, at least, not the way that you do. Even Cruise Control will not work unless you are prepared and fully ready to claim what you deserve: your best life and best health.

Your success depends on your long-term commitment, so are you ready to let go of your old, fat, and unhealthy body, and upgrade to an optimum model of health? The five commitments that you will need to strictly abide by are: (1) do not pledge to the product, rather pledge to the process (2) do not commit to a diet, rather commit to a lifestyle (3) be positive (4) be the driver, not the passenger, and (5) do not isolate yourself.

What to Expect

It is true that you can drop up to 30 pounds in the first five weeks on Cruise Control, but you need to understand that not all of the weight will come from loss of fat, it is more likely that only about ten to fifteen per cent of that weight will come from fat loss. Much of the rest will come from water retention related to inflammation. The other source of weight loss is what can be termed as "false fat" which is simply waste matter that is trapped inside your body. Regardless of where the weight loss comes from though, the good thing is that you will definitely get slimmer. Fiber is an important element your body needs in order to flush out waste from it, when you apply the required tips, you will feel fantastic and renewed.

Have Goals

Goal setting is a fundamental perquisite for success. It is more than mere wishful thinking. The success of your goal depends on your beliefs, desires, and a deep want for a specific wish to come true. Goal setting will help you expand and grow. Your reasons and motives should come first in any goal setting endeavor. Why? Because the more detailed and descriptive you are about your reasons for wanting to achieve your goal, the more strengthened your resolve to achieve it will be.

To be successful on Cruise Control, you must determine your goal or goals, investigate your motivation, and lastly, you will need to make a weekly review of your progress as this will spur you on towards a greater level of commitment.

Strategies to Motivate and Win

Even when we hit life's road blocks, these tips keep me and countless of clients moving forward. The first of these tips is for you to:

(i) create and use affirmations as your thoughts eventually become your action. You also need to:

(ii) design a vision board. This includes visual aids relating to your goal that keeps you motivated. You will also need to:

(iii) work on your kitchen, by making sure that the types of food that you shouldn't eat are not available there. Other tips include:

(iv) create an emotionally nourishing eating area,

(v) keep a daily motivation tracker, and

(vi) rally your support system etc.

Tips on Staying Motivated When Emotional Eating Calls

One of the first things you need to do when tempted to fill emotional holes with food is to identify the emotion, you will then need to actually feel the feeling as this equips you to handle it subsequently. You might also need to call a trusted friend and tell them about what and how you feel.

CHAPTER 5: YOUR FOUR-WEEK PLAN

KEY TAKEAWAYS

1. Commitment is needed in order to guarantee success.

2. You can live your life without limitations while on Cruise Control.

3. Sleep is an important part of the burn zone.

4. Drink plenty of water.

5. Consume lots of vegetables.

SUMMARY

Apart from letting you know that commitment is vital in achieving success with Cruise Control, I will also share with you, five commitments that you will need to make in order to guarantee success on Cruise Control. This chapter also lets you know how to have a transition after your fourth week into the fifth week and beyond.

Choose Your Gear

How you go about organizing your zone preparations over the next four weeks depends on the decisions you make. Some people tell me that they would need a measure of flexibility, while others just want to follow a detailed plan that does not involve making any decision on their own. Whatever your style is, I've got some options for you.

Follow My Meal Planner

This option is an option that I often recommend for people with busy schedules who are in need of a guaranteed plan. The meal planner is an apt description of Cruise Control. All that you need to do is simply follow each meal in the meal planner just as it is.

Choose foods that are approved by Cruise Control

From the list of foods that are approved by Cruise Control, you can create your own recipes based on how you're feeling that day. But don't forget to limit the boost foods to your boost zone hours only.

Make Cruise Control Recipes

I will be providing you with many recipes for snacks, meals, beverages, and treats. You can replace any snack, meal, or beverage on the food planners with any of these recipes.

Mix and Match

This part gives you freedom for flexibility, if you find that you like the exact meal plan of one week and yet really love several of my recipes, and want to add them to your boost line-up, then go for it! Remember that it is advisable that you pick the options that you love since that is what makes this lifestyle enjoyable.

Automate Your Schedule

When incorporating a new lifestyle plan, automation is key to success. Begin by deciding on the eight and sixteen hours boost and burn zones respectively, which you think will work best for you. Perhaps you are the type of person in the habit of getting up very early in the morning and eating immediately, the thought of continuing your burn zone once you are up and going might scare you. You might want to start your boost zone early in the day and also end it early – meaning an early dinner and you might then want to have burn zone tea or some other treat in the early hours of the evening. It is true that our schedule is usually not exactly the same from day to day, yet, the more consistent and specific you are, the better.

Don't Change Your Life

Ensure that you do not change your life while trying to fit into Cruise Control, this point cannot be overemphasized. There is simply no need to. You can continue to enjoy your life with no limitation while on Cruise Control. You don't need to force a specific boost or burn if there is a specific occasion to celebrate. Celebrate if you must, but do not forget that you are the driver here. So, all you need to do is to simply increase your next burn zone or start all over when you are ready.

Shop, Prepare, and Eat

Now that you are all geared up and have made some decisions about how to organize your boost and burn zones for the next four weeks, all you need now is to let me take the lead.

CHAPTER 6: RECIPES

BURN ZONE BREAKFAST BEVERAGE RECIPES

Cruiser Coffee

NOTE: You have a choice of MCT oil or coconut oil and a choice between ghee and grass-fed butter for this recipe. A few things to remember: (i) if your blended mixture is too hot, then exercise due care as you open the blender and a s you pour. (ii) You can also make this recipe with any tea or any other decaf beverage. This recipe is for 1 cup. The preparation time for this recipe is about 3 minutes.
INGREDIENTS: 1 cup of coffee; 1 or 2 tablespoons coconut oil or MCT oil; a pinch of Himalayan salt; 1 or 2 tablespoons of ghee or unsalted butter (both grass-fed).
DIRECTIONS: (1) Put all the ingredients in an immersion blender. (2) Blend until mixture becomes creamy. (2) Enjoy!

Cinna's Coffee

NOTE: The Cinnas Coffee is a breakfast beverage so delicious it'll wash your sins way! Just kiddin'. This beverage has a coffee and cinnamon spice mix as its signature ingredient. You may top your Cinnas Coffee with whipped cream, but whipped cream is optional. This Cinnas Coffee recipe is for 1 cup. The preparation time for this recipe is about 3 minutes.

INGREDIENTS: 1 cup of coffee; 1 or 2 tablespoons of coconut oil or MCT oil; ½ or 1 tablespoon of a program-approved sweetener; ¼ or ½ teaspoon of ground cinnamon; and whipped cream (but this is optional).

DIRECTIONS: (1) Except for the whipped cream (that is, if you are using whipped cream), put all the ingredients in an immersion blender. (2) Blend until mixture becomes creamy. (3) Top it up with whipped cream if you choose. (4) Enjoy!

Hot Cocoffee

NOTE: The Cocoffee is a great-tasting, beautiful breakfast beverage with a coffee and cocoa mix as its signature ingredient. You may top your Cocoffee with whipped cream, but whipped cream is optional. This Cocoffee recipe is for 1 cup. The preparation time for this Cocoffee recipe is about 3 minutes.

INGREDIENTS: 1 cup of coffee; 2 tablespoons of cocoa powder (unsweetened); 1 or 2 tablespoons of MCT oil or coconut oil; ½ or 1 cup of almond milk (unsweetened); ½ or 1 tablespoon of a program-approved sweetener; ½ or 1 teaspoon of pure vanilla extract; and Whipped cream (but this is optional).

DIRECTIONS: (1) Except for the whipped cream (that is, if you are using whipped cream), put all the ingredients in an immersion blender. (2) Blend until mixture becomes creamy. (3) Top it up with whipped cream if you choose. (4) Enjoy!

Coconutty Coffee

NOTE: The Coconutty Coffee is another delicious and exquisite breakfast beverage with a coffee and coconut milk mix as its signature ingredient. This Coconutty Coffee recipe is for 1 cup. The preparation time for this this recipe is about 3 minutes.

INGREDIENTS: 1 cup of coffee; 2 tablespoons of coconut milk (unsweetened); 1 or 2 tablespoons coconut oil or MCT oil; ½ or 1 tablespoon of a program-approved sweetener; 1 or 2 tablespoons of ghee or unsalted butter (both grass-fed).

DIRECTIONS: (1) Put all the ingredients in an immersion blender. (2) Blend until mixture becomes creamy. (2) Enjoy!

Butter-Up Tea

NOTE: The Butter-Up Tea is a great-tasting and satisfying breakfast beverage with loose-leaf black tea, butter and heavy cream as its signature ingredients. This Butter-Up Tea recipe serves 2. The preparation time for this recipe is about 5 to 10 minutes.

INGREDIENTS: 2 tablespoons of loose-leaf black tea (either regular or decaf is fine); 2 tablespoons of butter (unsalted and grass-fed); ½ cup of heavy cream; and ¼ teaspoon of salt.

DIRECTIONS: (1) Bring 2 cups of water to boil in a medium saucepan, over medium-high heat and reduce the heat when the water has boiled. (2) Simmer the 2 tablespoons of loose-leaf black tea in the boiled water for about 2 or 3 minutes. (3) Strain and cool slightly. (4) Add the butter, salt and cream and whisk for about 1 minute until it's frothy. (4) Enjoy!

BURN ZONE TREATS RECIPES

Either-Or Chocolatty Mousse

NOTE: This recipe for the Either-Or Chocolatty Mousse is for 2 servings. This recipe can be served either cold or hot. The preparation time is about 10 to 15 minutes (if serving cold) or about 5 minutes (if serving hot).
INGREDIENTS: Chocolate pudding and pie filling (Simply Delish brand recommended); and 2 to 3 cups of heavy cream.
DIRECTIONS: (1) Beat the pudding mix with the heavy cream in a medium bowl for about 2 to 3 minutes. (2) Place the mixture in the refrigerator for about 10 minutes so it can chill and thicken. Or for hot pudding, heat the pudding mix in a microwave for about 30 seconds. (3) Pour the mousse into a serving dish. (4) Enjoy!

Buttery Goodry Icedrops

NOTE: This recipe for the Buttery Goodry Icedrops is for 9 servings. The preparation time is about 4 hours because you have to let it freeze into yummy, goody ice cubes!

INGREDIENTS: ½ or 1 tablespoons of butter (unsalted and grass-fed); ½ or 1 cup of coconut oil; ½ or 1 teaspoon of cinnamon; 1 tablespoon of liquid stevia; and ¼ teaspoon of sea salt

DIRECTIONS: (1) Microwave the butter in a microwave-safe dish for about 30 to 45 seconds (microwave on high) until butter melts. (2) Mix the cinnamon, coconut oil, stevia and sea salt in a bowl. (3) Whisk the mixture until creamy, then pour into several compartments in an ice cube tray. (4) Leave the ice cube tray in the freezer until frozen (about 4 hours). (5) Remove ice cube tray from freezer and pop out your delicious Buttery Goodry Icedrops! (6) Enjoy!

Vanichia Pudding

NOTE: The Vanichia Pudding is a delicious and exquisite treat which has chia seeds, coconut milk and vanilla extract as its signature ingredients. This recipe is for 6 servings. The preparation time is at least 1 hour because you have to refrigerate the goodness!

INGREDIENTS: ½ or ¾ cup of chia seeds; 1 ½ or 2 teaspoons of vanilla extract; 15 ounces of full-fat coconut milk; and ⅓ or ¼ cup of a program-approved sweetener.

DIRECTIONS: (1) In a bowl, mix the chia seeds with 1 ½ cups of hot water. (2) Add the full-fat coconut milk, sweetener and vanilla extract. Beat thoroughly with a spoon. (3) Separate into 6 equal parts and pour into 6 bowls or cups of your choice.

(4) Refrigerate for at least an hour or overnight as you choose. (5) And enjoy!

Strawberry Cream Pops

NOTE: This recipe is for 6 servings. The preparation time is at least 4 hours because you have to freeze it!

INGREDIENTS: 1 box of Strawberry Jel Dessert (Simply Delish brand recommended); and 1 cup of heavy cream.

DIRECTIONS: (1) Bring ½ cup of water to boil in a small saucepan (medium-high heat). (2) Remove the boiling water from heat. (3) Mix the Strawberry Jel Dessert into the boiled water until it dissolves. (4) Pour into a blender. (5) Add the heavy cream into the blender. (6) Blend until creamy smooth. (7) Pour the mixture inside popsicle molds. (8) Place in the freezer until frozen (about 4 hours). (9) Remove from freezer, pop out your delicious Strawberry Cream Pops! (10) Enjoy!

BOOST ZONE MEALS RECIPES

Either-Or Omelet

NOTE: This is a very simple "omelet" recipe, but don't be fooled because it tastes so ***delicioso***! Note that you can substitute the ham with any other cooked protein, and that you can also substitute the spinach with kale or any other greens of your choice. This recipe is for 1 serving. The preparation time is about 5 minutes.

INGREDIENTS: 2 big eggs; 2 or 3 slices ham - diced; ½ bell pepper - diced; ¼ or ½ cup of fresh spinach; pinch of ground black pepper; and pinch of salt.

DIRECTIONS: (1) Put all the ingredients together in a microwave-safe mug. (2) Cook for about 2 to 4 minutes. (3) Stir halfway as it cooks and do not allow the egg to bubble over (4) Enjoy!

Good-Pot Shrimp Alfredo

NOTE: This recipe is for 4 servings. The preparation time is about 8 to 12 minutes. Remember not to overcook the shrimp. It's more delicious when not overcooked!

INGREDIENTS: 1 pound of shrimp (raw); 4 ounces of cubed cream cheese; 1 or 1 ½ tablespoon of salted, grass-fed butter; ½ or ¾ cup of whole milk; ½ or ¾ cup of Parmesan cheese (shredded); 4 to 6 sun-dried whole tomatoes (cut them into strips); ¼ or ½ cup of spinach or baby kale; ½ or 1 teaspoon of dried basil; ½ or 1 tablespoon of garlic powder; and 1 teaspoon of salt.

DIRECTIONS: (1) Melt the salted, grass-fed butter in a big skillet over medium heat. (2) Cook shrimp in the skillet for about 30 seconds over medium-low heat. (3) Turn the shrimp over and cook the other side until it's somewhat pink. (4) Add the milk and the cream cheese cubes and stir until the cream cheese melts and no lumps are present. (5) Add the basil, garlic powder and salt and stir in properly. (6) Add the Parmesan cheese and stir in. Allow the sauce to simmer until it begins to thicken. (7) Fold in the spinach or baby kale and the sun-dried tomatoes. (8) It's ready! Serve and enjoy!

Cruiser-Rave Portobello Mini-Pizza

NOTE: This is a favorite of your fellow followers of the Cruise Control Program. Give it a try. It just tastes ***grrreat***! This recipe is for 2 servings. The preparation time is about 15 to 25 minutes.

INGREDIENTS: 2 big portobello caps (remove stems); 10 to 15 black Kalamata olives; 1 cup of Italian blend cheese (shredded); 1 tablespoon of capers; ½ or ¾ cup of pesto; Pinch of Basil (for garnish, optional); Pinch of crushed red pepper flakes (for garnish, optional).

DIRECTIONS: (1) Preheat oven to 375 degrees Fahrenheit. (2) Put the mushrooms on a rimmed baking sheet. (3) Spread the pesto in each mushroom. (4) Add cheese to the centers of the mushrooms. (5) Top with capers and olives. (6) Bake for 10 to 20 minutes or until the mushrooms start to soften and the cheese starts to bubble. (7) Sprinkle with basil and crushed red pepper flakes (optional) or place in the refrigerator for up to one day and reheat when ready to serve. (8) Enjoy!

Tunachia Salad

NOTE: This recipe is for 2 servings. The preparation time is about 15 to 25 minutes.

INGREDIENTS: ½ cup of mayonnaise; 1 tablespoon of lemon juice; 1 or 2 tablespoons of EVOO (extra-virgin olive oil); 1 tablespoon of parsley (chopped); ¼ cup of chia seeds; ¼ teaspoon of salt; ¼ teaspoon of ground black pepper; 1 head of romaine lettuce

1 cucumber (sliced); 1 onion, sliced; 1 five-ounce can of tuna (drained); 10 to 15 black Kalamata olives (sliced); 4 big eggs (hard-boiled).

DIRECTIONS: (1) In a bowl, whisk the lemon juice, mayonnaise, parsley, olive oil, pepper and salt until blended. (2) Fold the lettuce leaves into a medium bowl. (3) Top the lettuce leaves with the tuna, onion, cucumber, olives and chia seeds. (4) Slice the eggs and add to the salad. (5) Add some of the dressing onto the salad. (6) Enjoy!

Turkey-in-a-Bento Box

NOTE: If you do not have a real bento box, you may use a rectangular plastic container to pack this lunch meal. This recipe is for 1 serving. The preparation time is about 5 to 10 minutes.

INGREDIENTS: 3 slices of deli turkey (no sugar added); 2 tablespoons of cream cheese; ¼ cup of Cheddar cheese or Colby Jack cheese (cubed); 1 teaspoon of ranch seasoning; ¼ or ½ cup of hazelnuts; ¼ or ½ cup of blackberries; ½ cucumber (sliced); ¼ or ½ red bell pepper (sliced).

DIRECTIONS: (1) Using a small bowl, mix the ranch seasoning and the cream cheese and until smooth. (2) Smear the cheese/seasoning mixture on the slices of turkey. (3) Top with the ball pepper and a slice of cucumber. (4) Roll it all up in the turkey and cut the rolled-up turkey in half. (5) Serve in a container along with the cheese, berries and nuts. (6) Enjoy!

Stir Fry in the Zone

NOTE: If you do not have the veggies used in this recipe, you may use any seasonal veggies of your choice. This recipe is for 6 servings. The preparation time is about 40 minutes.

INGREDIENTS: 2 teaspoons of chopped fresh ginger root (divided); 1 small head of broccoli (cut into florets); ¼ or ½ red bell pepper; ¾ cup of carrots (julienned); ½ cup of onion (chopped)' ¼ cup of snow peas; (sliced); ½ cup of green beans (halved); 1 tablespoon of cornstarch; 1 clove of garlic (crushed); ¼ cup of vegetable oil (divided); 2 tablespoons soy sauce; ½ tablespoon of salt; 3 tablespoons of water.

DIRECTIONS: (1) In a big bowl, blend garlic, cornstarch, 2 tablespoons of vegetable oil and 1 teaspoon of ginger, until the cornstarch dissolves. (2) Add the snow peas, broccoli, green beans, red bell pepper, and carrots, tossing lightly as you add the vegetables. (3) Heat the remaining oil in a big skillet over medium heat. (4) Cook the vegetables in the oil for two minutes. Keep stirring constantly. (5) Add water and soy sauce and keep stirring. (6) Add the remaining ginger, salt and onion. (7) Keep stirring as you cook, until the vegetables are somewhat tender (but still crisp). (8) Remove from heat. Serve and enjoy!

BLT Ranch Wrap

NOTE: This recipe is for 1 serving. The preparation time is about 3 to 5 minutes.

INGREDIENTS: For the Ranch Dressing: 1 tablespoon of mayonnaise; 1 teaspoon of dried parsley; ¼ teaspoon of onion powder; ¼ teaspoon of garlic powder; 1 ½ teaspoon of lemon juice; Pinch of black pepper (freshly ground); Pinch of salt. **For the Lettuce Wrap:** 2 to 4 leaves of leaf lettuce; 2 or 3 slices of cooked bacon; ½ small avocado (sliced); 2 to 4 tomatoes, sliced.

DIRECTIONS: (1) In a bowl, mix all the ingredients for the ranch dressing together. (2) Then arrange the lettuce leaves, slightly overlapping, but in a single layer. (3) Drizzle the lettuce leaves with the ranch dressing. (4) Top the lettuce leaves with bacon, avocado and tomato. (5) Roll the lettuce leaves. Tuck in the edges as you do so. (6) Cut in the wrap in half after. Ensure wrap is tight and properly secured). (7) Enjoy!

Cashew Chicken Breast

NOTE: This recipe is for 3 servings. The preparation time is about 30 minutes.

INGREDIENTS: ¼ cup of raw cashews; 3 boneless, skinless chicken breasts; 1 large green bell pepper; 1 tablespoon of green onions; ½ large white onion; 2

tablespoons of coconut oil; 1 tablespoon of garlic (minced); 1 tablespoon of rice wine vinegar; 1 tablespoon of sesame oil; 1 teaspoon of sesame seeds; 1 teaspoon of chili garlic sauce; ¾ teaspoon of ginger (ground); black pepper (freshly ground); salt.

DIRECTIONS: (1) Toast the cashews in a pan over low heat for 6 to 10 minutes. Remove from heat and set aside. (2) Dice the chicken breasts into chunks. (3) Cut the white onion and the bell pepper into chunks. (4) Add the coconut oil to the pan. (5) Add the chicken to the pan. (6). Cook the chicken in the coconut oil over high heat for about 5 minutes. (7) Add the white onions, bell pepper, garlic, ginger, green onions, chili garlic sauce. (8) Add pinch(es) of the salt and the ground black pepper to taste. (9) Cook for about 3 to 4 minutes. (10) Add the cashews and the rice wine vinegar and cook for 3 to 4 more minutes. (11) Place in serving bowl. Drizzle with the sesame oil and top with the sesame seeds. (12) Enjoy!

Goat Cheese & Ham Frittata

NOTE: This recipe is for 6 servings. The preparation time is about 25 to 30 minutes.

INGREDIENTS: 6 ounces of smoked ham (chopped); 6 ounces of goat cheese; ½ cup of Cheddar cheese (grated); 8 big eggs; 1/2 cup of broccoli florets (chopped); ½ red bell pepper (chopped); ½ onion (diced); ½ pound asparagus (trim the ends and cut into two-inch pieces); ½ teaspoon of garlic powder; ½ cup of heavy cream; 1 tablespoon of EVOO (extra-virgin olive oil).

DIRECTIONS: (1) Preheat oven to 400 degrees Fahrenheit. (2) Heat the olive oil in a skillet (nonstick oven-proof) over medium heat. (3) Add the asparagus, onion, bell pepper and broccoli and cook the mix for about 3 to 4 minutes. (4) In a bowl, whisk the eggs, the ham and the cream together. (5) Add the Cheddar cheese and garlic powder to the bowl and stir. (6) Pour the egg-mixture contents of the bowl into the same pan that contains the asparagus, broccoli, onion, etc. (7) Top it up with the goat cheese (crumbled). (8) Put the pan into the oven. Cook for 14 to 16 minutes. (9) Cut the frittata into wedges. (10) Serve and enjoy!

BOOST ZONE SNACKS RECIPES

Golden Cheese & Cabbage Chips

NOTE: This recipe is for 6 servings. The preparation time is about 35 to 45 minutes.
INGREDIENTS: 1 big head of cabbage; 2 teaspoons of EVOO (extra-virgin olive oil); ½ cup of Parmesan cheese (grated); salt; black pepper (freshly ground).
DIRECTIONS: (1) Preheat oven to 450 degrees Fahrenheit. (2) Set 1 wire rack inside each of 2 rimmed baking-sheets. (3) Cut the cabbage leaves into big pieces. Discard the parts of the ribs that are thickest. (4) Add the olive oil and Parmesan cheese on the cabbage leaves and toss. (5) Season with pepper and salt. (6) Arrange on the wire racks in a

single layer. (7) Bake for 30 to 40 minutes or until the chips are crispy and golden. (8) Serve and enjoy!

Cheese & Broccoli Bread Rendezvous

NOTE: This recipe is for 8 servings. The preparation time is about 40 to 45 minutes.

INGREDIENTS: 3 cups of riced broccoli; 1½ cups of mozzarella (shredded); ½ cup of Parmesan cheese (grated); 1 big egg; ½ teaspoon of oregano (dried); 1 clove of garlic (minced); black pepper (freshly ground); salt

DIRECTIONS: (1) Preheat oven to 425 degrees Fahrenheit. (2) Line parchment paper on a rimmed baking-sheet. (3) Microwave the riced broccoli to steam in a microwave-safe bowl for about 1 minute. (4) Use a paper towel to soak up the moisture from the broccoli. (5) Put the broccoli in a bowl. Add the Parmesan cheese, the egg and the garlic. Then add 1 cup of the mozzarella cheese (reserve the remaining ½ cup of mozzarella). (6) Season with salt, pepper and oregano. (7) Place the dough on the baking sheet. Shape into round, thin crust. (8) Bake until golden (about 20 minutes). (9) Top the dough with the remaining ½ cup of mozzarella cheese and bake until the crust gets crispy and the cheese melts (about 10 minutes). (10) Serve the goodness and enjoy!

Pepperoni Pizza Chips

NOTE: This recipe is for 7 servings. The preparation time is about 15 minutes. For the pepperoni, you may choose to use the gluten-free, nitrate-free variety of turkey pepperoni (such as the Applegate brand). They are healthy and they taste great.

INGREDIENTS: 6 ounces of pepperoni (sliced); and 2 cups of mozzarella cheese (shredded).

DIRECTIONS: (1) Preheat oven to 400 degrees Fahrenheit. (2) Arrange the slices of pepperoni closely together (in batches of 4), on a rimmed baking-sheet. (3) Bake for about 4 minutes. Spread the cheese on top and bake for about another 4 minutes (until the cheese gets crispy and melted. (4) Put the chips on paper towels and let them cool for about 5 minutes. (5) Its ready! Serve the goodness and enjoy!

Cream Cheese Celery Boat-load

NOTE: This recipe is for 4 servings. The preparation time is about 5 minutes. This is a great on-the-go snack!

INGREDIENTS: 2 ½ one-ounce packages of cream cheese; 12 stalks celery (rinsed); and 1 ½ teaspoon of "Everything bagel" seasoning.

DIRECTIONS: (1) Cut each stalk of celery into 3 sections. (2) Stuff the stalks of celery with cream-cheese. (3) Sprinkle the "Everything bagel" seasoning on the celery stalks. (4) It's ready! Serve and enjoy!

Caulieese Muffins

NOTE: The Caulieese Muffin is a delicious snack with cauliflower and cheese as its signature ingredients. This recipe is for 8 servings. The preparation time is about 45 to 55 minutes.

INGREDIENTS: 1 big cauliflower (chopped); 3 ounces of cream cheese; 2 cups of sharp Cheddar cheese (shredded); 1 ½ cup of heavy cream; 2 big eggs (beaten); black pepper (freshly ground); ½ teaspoons of onion powder; non-stick cooking spray,

DIRECTIONS: (1) Preheat oven to 350 degrees Fahrenheit. (2) Spray the non-stick spray on a muffin tin. (3) Boil a big pot of water over medium high heat. (4) Add the cauliflower and let it boil for about 8 to 12 minutes or until it's tender. Then drain the cauliflower. (5) In a saucepan, over low heat, cook the cream cheese and the cream, stirring constantly for about 5 minutes. (6) Add the pepper and onion powder. (7) Add the cauliflower, the eggs and 1 cup of shredded Cheddar and keep stirring until its creamy and smooth. (8) Spoon the mixture into the muffin tin, then sprinkle with the ¾ cup of shredded Cheddar cheese that is remaining. (9) Bake for about 20 minutes. (10) Let it cool for about 15 minutes before you remove them from the muffin pan. (11) It's ready! Enjoy!

The Cruiser Everything Bagel Topping (aka The Fierce)

NOTE: Here's a bonus snack recipe for ya! This is the Cruiser Everything Bagel Topping also known as "The Fierce", not because it's peppery or anything like that, but just because when you put it on all kinds of foods, it makes 'em beautiful, interesting and so **snackilicious**! You can top your salads, avocado toasts, hummus, tofu, muffins, popcorn, chips, porridge, broccoli, etc., with The Fierce. This recipe makes 10 tablespoons-servings. The preparation time is about 5 minutes. If necessary, store in an air-tight container in an extra dry environment.

INGREDIENTS: 4 tablespoons of white sesame seeds; 4 tablespoons of poppy seeds; 2 teaspoons of chia seeds; 3 tablespoons of dehydrated onion (chopped); 2 tablespoon of dehydrated garlic (minced); ¾ tablespoon of flaked sea-salt.

DIRECTIONS: (1) Throw all the ingredients into a jar. (2) Hold the jar with both hands and shake it, baby! Just shake it like you just don't care! When it's all mixed up nice, then it's ready to use on your favorite foods! (3) Enjoy!

BOOST ZONE DESSERTS RECIPES

Chocolatty Avo Pops

NOTE: The Chocolatty Avo Pops is a yummy dessert recipe with chocolate chips and avocados as its signature ingredients. This recipe is for 10 servings. The preparation time is at least 6 hours up to overnight because you have to freeze the popsicles to get them yummy, yummy, yummy!

INGREDIENTS: 3 ripe avocados; 1 cup of dark chocolate chips (at least 55% cocoa); 1 ½ tablespoons of coconut oil; 1 cup of coconut milk; ⅓ cup of lime juice; 3 tablespoons of program-approved sweetener.

DIRECTIONS: (1) In a blender, blend avocados, coconut milk, sweetener and lime juice until creamy and smooth, then pour into popsicle molds. (2) Freeze the popsicle molds overnight or until the molds are firm (for 6 hours, at least). (3) Microwave the coconut oil and the dark chocolate-chips in a microwave-safe bowl, until melted. (4) Remove from heat and let it cool. (5) Dip the frozen popsicles in the chocolate goodness and serve! (6) Enjoy!

Choco "More!" Pudding

NOTE: This is a beautiful dessert you can have on-the-go. It also makes a great-tasting dip for your vegetables! This recipe is for 2 servings. The preparation time is about 3 to 5 minutes.
INGREDIENTS: 3 ounces of whole-fat plain yogurt; 1 big avocado (overripe); 2 teaspoons of cinnamon; ½ cup unsweetened cocoa powder; ¼ cup Cruise Control-friendly sweetener; ¼ teaspoon of pure vanilla extract; and ¼ teaspoon of cayenne pepper.
DIRECTIONS: (1) Throw all the ingredients in a blender and blend until creamy and smooth. (2) Spoon equal measures into 2 bowls and serve. (3) Enjoy!

The Malibu Million-Dollar Handshake Milkshake

NOTE: This is an adaptation of a great smoothie that you can get at SunLife Organics, in Malibu, California. It's just so outta-here delicious! You gotta try it! This recipe is for 1 serving. The preparation time is about 3 to 5 minutes.

INGREDIENTS: ¾ cup of almond milk (unsweetened); 1 ½ teaspoon of cacao powder (raw); 1 ½ scoops of vanilla whey-protein (grass-fed); 1 teaspoon of chia seeds; 1 tablespoon of MCT oil; 1 tablespoon of cashew butter (raw); 1 tablespoon of a program-approved sweetener.

DIRECTIONS: (1) Throw all the ingredients in a blender and blend until creamy and smooth. (2) Enjoy!

The Nutty Chocolatty Macadamit (!) Parfait

NOTE: This is a very tasty parfait! This recipe is for 1 serving. The preparation time is about 2 to 3 minutes.

INGREDIENTS: 1 one-ounce packet of salted, chocolate, macadamia nut butter (FBOMB brand recommended); 3 tablespoons of macadamia nuts; 5 ounces of whole-fat plain yogurt.

DIRECTIONS: (1) Open the 5-ounce container of whole-fat plain yogurt. (2) Squeeze the packet of salted, chocolate, macadamia nut butter (FBOMB brand recommended) into the container of yogurt. (3) Stir the mixture properly. (4) Top it up with the macadamia nuts. (5) Its ready! Serve and enjoy!

The Almond Butter-Up "Pacesetter" Cookies

NOTE: These cookies are just grrreat! Give 'em a try, you'll like 'em! This recipe is for 15 servings. The preparation time is about 20 to 25 minutes.

INGREDIENTS: 1 ½ cups of natural almond butter; 1 big egg; ¾ teaspoon of cinnamon (ground); 1 teaspoon of pure vanilla extract; ½ cup of program-approved sweetener; and ¼ teaspoon of salt.

DIRECTIONS: (1) Preheat oven to 350 degrees Fahrenheit. (2) Line parchment paper on a baking-sheet. (3) Mix the almond butter and the sweetener together in a bowl until creamy and smooth. (4) Mix in the vanilla extract, cinnamon, salt and the egg. Stir thoroughly until creamy and smooth. (5) Scoop the mixture in equal measures into 15 cookies. (6) Put the balls of dough 2-inches apart on the prepared baking sheet. (7) Flatten the dough balls with a fork, forming a crisscross pattern. (8) Bake the dough balls until their bottoms become slightly browned (for about 10 to 12 minutes). (9) Let the cookies cool the baking-sheet for about 5 minutes. (10) Its ready! Serve and enjoy!

Blessed Mug Cake

NOTE: Why blessed? Because we say so! And it'll bring you good luck, happiness and whatever good thing your heart desires (honest)! Plus, it tastes like pure blessing! So, what are you waiting for? Go on! Make it and eat it! You'll love it! This recipe is for 1 serving. The preparation time is about 3 to 5 minutes.

INGREDIENTS: 1 big egg; 2 tablespoons of almond-flour; 2 tablespoons of butter; ¼ teaspoon of pure vanilla extract; ½ teaspoon of baking-powder; ¼ teaspoon of nutmeg; ¼ teaspoon of cinnamon (and more for serving); 7 drops of stevia (liquid); 1 tablespoon of program-approved sweetener; whipped cream (but this is optional).

DIRECTIONS: (1) Mix the almond flour, butter, egg, liquid stevia, sweetener, vanilla, nutmeg, cinnamon, and baking powder, all together in a microwave-safe mug. (2) Microwave on high temperature for about 1 minute. (3) Remove mug from microwave and turn upside down on a flat plate. Remove the cake. (4) Top the cake with a dash of cinnamon. (5) Also top with some whipped cream (but the whipped cream is optional). (6) Its ready! Enjoy!

CHAPTER 7: THE EXERCISE EFFECT

KEY TAKEAWAYS

1. Aim for exercises that get your heart thumping.
2. Exercise improves your mood and physical health.
3. You should aim to exercise near the end of the burn zone, in the morning.
4. Muscle burns fat.
5. Burning melts fat faster.

SUMMARY

Does movement automatically translate into actual workout? The truth is that all kinds of movement is beneficial for your health. Yet, it is best that you go for the kinds of exercises that gets your heart thumping or the types of exercises that aim at building muscles. These types of exercises will boost your mood, fight disease, help build your cognitive abilities, lower the risk of heart diseases and decrease body and back pain. No matter the situation your body is currently in, perhaps you are old or you have failed so many times, and you now feel that workout is simply not for you. None of that is true, you can always work out!

I will introduce to you, a type of workout that uses only two moves a day, and will take you just eight minutes to complete. This workout will make you lose about two pounds of fat a week.

Learning to Exercise from Animals
There is something we can learn about exercise by closely observing animals. Watch the way your dog moves or pay close attention to an animal show on the TV. Do you ever see animals jog? No, they don't, all you see is cheetahs' zooming after gazelles or similar things. The point is that **at our primal level, neither humans nor animals were designed for low intensity, extended movements.** We are made to either walk or sprint.

Movement: A Medicine for the Mind
How do you feel after an unusually active day? While you might be sore and tired, you will also have that kind of good tired feeling that comes from being active, there is a certain kind of calm, serenity, and energy that you get to feel as a result. When it comes to its effect on mood and physical health, exercise is as powerful as medicine. Some of the benefits of proper exercise are: mood improvement, relief from stress, enhanced memory, and a natural high.

Short Bursts of Exercise Boosts Your Burn!

When health experts recommend that you get an hour of moderate exercise, they do so with regards to helping you to improve your health and to maintain your weight generally. That recommendation is never aimed at helping you to seriously burn off fat! Based on this, my eight-minute workout does not aim to maintain your weight generally, instead, it is directed at helping you to burn fat, to reduce your weight. It provides additional boost to your fat burning engine which should be already revved up. In other words, exercise plus your burn zone eating will absolutely get the weight off you! So, my eight-minute workout provides the extra boost that will actually ramp up your rapid weight loss including rapid belly burning.

The role of catecholamine in boosting your burn

Catecholamines are a group of neurotransmitters and hormones that the body pumps out in response to stress, and they boost fat burning in your body, how do they do that? Adrenaline. They are generally activated by the triggering of your fight-or-flight response. You perceive danger, adrenaline is released, your digestion slows down and your heart speeds up… your body is given a burst of energy, and you are ready to battle.

Catecholamines are also activated and release adrenaline in response to a certain type of exercise (the HIIT or high intensity interval training). HIIT is a type of exercise that requires that you alternate intervals of all-out effort. It might require that you sprint at your fastest, and then following it with moderate intensity exercise, such as a brisk walk.

Instead of spending hours at the gym, the Cruise Control workout makes use of alternate periods of intense but short anaerobic movements with a recovery period that is less intense. You can be sure that the process is not complicated.

Principles behind the Cruise Control Workout
The first principle governing the Cruise Control workout deals with the timing of the exercise. In order to achieve maximum fat burning, I recommend that you exercise near the end of your Burn zone, that is, in the morning. The timing is perfect since it is the time when your body starts burning the limited glycogen in your liver.

CHAPTER 8: YOUR CRUISE CONTROL WORKOUT

KEY TAKEAWAYS

1. Aim for 80% to 90% of your capable intensity during the high-intensity movement.

2. Moving between high intensity exercises speeds up lactic acid removal.

3. Focus on the quality of your moves, not just quantity.

4. Get enough rest.

5. Fuel your workout by rehydrating and getting enough electrolytes.

SUMMARY

The Cruise Control program works with the alternating high-intensity, low-intensity workout that maximizes weight loss. This workout regimen requires only about eight minutes a day! So altogether, it will take forty minutes a week at five times per week and eight minutes a day. That is all you need in order to activate the powerful neurotransmitters and fat-mobilizing hormones that will burn off your belly fat in the most effective manner. All you need is participation and a high level of commitment.

This workout regime works in a simple way. All you need to do is warm up for a few minutes. You will alternate a one-minute low-intensity move with a one-minute high-intensity move for a total of eight minutes. You will cool off for some minutes and simply continue with your day. That is all.

High-Intensity Moves
The aim here is to temporarily stress your body in such a way that it can burn fat in an eight-minute workout. Ensure that you make these moves at an intensity level of 80-95 per cent of the total energy output of your body. ***Ensure that in just that one minute, your muscles are fatigued and your heart rate is pumping fast.*** In order to accurately mimic the movement of our ancestors while hunting, you will need to engage all your large muscles, and many of the small ones in the exercise. At this level of intensity, you shouldn't be able to talk. And at the end of the eight minutes, you should, and will be sweating profusely.

Some High-Intensity Moves
Exercise No. 1: Intermittent Overhead Press
Exercise No. 2: Overhead March
Exercise No. 3: Alternating Gate Squats
Exercise No. 4: Skater Glute Pulse

Exercise No. 5: Standing Push-Ups with Shoulder Taps
Exercise No. 6: YTW Exercise
Exercise No. 7: Stir the Pot
Exercise No. 8: Alternating Prisoner Twist March
Exercise No. 9: Squat Plus Toe Press
Exercise No. 10: Alternating Thigh March

The Role of the Low-Intensity Moves
Continually moving between high-intensity exercises helps speed up the removal of lactic acid from the body and lower bloodstream acidity. Keeping you're your body moving gives the energy you need in order to carry out the next high-intensity interval. These exercises should be done in a controlled manner, focusing on contracting the muscles in each move. Try to be at a 6 or 7 intensity level during active recovery.

Room for Flexibility
If you feel that a move is either too difficult or too easy for you, all you need to do is modify it. There is no rigid rule here, your goal is to tap into the intensity in order to ensure that your body burns fat. Also, if you start with modifications, you will later be able to add extra minutes to your workout.

You can also reduce the 60 seconds to 30 seconds if you think that you need a gradual approach. You will feel, and get stronger as the weeks roll by and you will soon master all the moves.

Also, if you want a harder workout because you feel like you are not reaching the 80 to 95 level of intensity, then ramp it up! Make your hands move more powerfully or explosively, add a hop or a jog. If you still don't feel that level of intensity, then you can go for as many rounds as you want.

Warming Up and Cooling Down

Before, and at the end of every workout, take a moment to move around and get your body ready for your workout and to go back down when you are done. Jog gently, walk in place, lift and lower your shoulders, circle your arms, lift and lower your knees, or simply dance around. Just move!

How To "Engage" Your Core While Exercising

When exercising try to engage your core or your muscles. So, what does that mean? It means engaging the muscles of your stomach, butt and back. They work together. Imagine that someone is about to punch you in the stomach. You would instinctively brace your stomach, back and butt muscles to take the punch, that is engaging your core. Do not let your belly to pooch out. Pull it in. And make sure you are in a good posture at all times. But do not limit the engagement of your muscles t only the muscles of your stomach, butt and back. Also "engage" or "brace" other muscles in your body. While exercising maintain good control and form. Do not flop around. Mind your posture and control your movements. In other words, engage your core!

Reward Yourself After Each Week of Workouts.

Be sure to reward yourself after every week of workouts. Treat yourself (e.g. to a massage, the movies, spa treatment, or a session of cryotherapy, etc.). Cryotherapy is outta this world! It's strange and exciting. Try it. It's also good for reducing inflammation, and for arthritis and or joint pain.

Rest Day and Alternative Activities

Take a day off and rest whenever you need it. But on your rest days, don't just laze around on the sofa. Instead do something that is fun but which still involves moving your body (bike rides, strolls, gardening, doing active domestic chores, etc.).

Rejuvenating and Recovering After A Workout

The best way to recover after intense exercising includes, first, hydrating and fueling yourself. That one is basic and the most important. Additionally, you can try things like getting sessions of natural light therapy - red light therapy (check this out its really cool!). Red light therapy counters fatigue, stimulates your cells and recharges your mitochondria. It is also good for joint mobility and strained or stiff muscles. It boosts collagen for fast healing and builds muscle strength. Other things you could also do on your rest days that involves you moving your body include: going for a walk, going for a bike ride, doing yoga, hiking, lifting weights, jump rope or jump around on the trampoline, play some pick-up basketball, go swimming, dancing. What about sweating it out in a sauna? Have I mentioned gardening?

Fueling Your Workout

While exercising and after exercising, make sure to rehydrate and get enough electrolytes. Intense exercise can cause you to sweat out too much electrolytes. You can keep hydrated by having a sports drink but make sure it's one that does not contain too much sugar (it's hard to find). But try one called LyteShow. It's natural. Some foods also can help you to fuel your body both pre-workout and post-workout.

For your ***PRE-WORKOUT, BURN ZONE*** hydration and fueling requirements, the following foods will foot the bill: Cruise Control Coffee; ginseng tea; matcha, green tea, and water that contains lemon.

For your ***PRE-WORKOUT, BOOST ZONE*** hydration and fueling requirements, the following foods will foot the bill: hard-boiled egg, avocado, nuts, protein shake, and jerky.

For your ***POST-WORKOUT, BURN ZONE*** hydration and fueling requirements, the following foods will come in handy: coffee, sparkling water, water, bone broth and black tea.

And for your ***POST-WORKOUT, BOOST ZONE*** hydration and fueling requirements, try the following foods: celery, broccoli, eggs, full-fat yogurt, and a vegetable smoothie.

CHAPTER 9: HEALTHY LIVING - ANYWHERE, ANYTIME

KEY TAKEAWAYS

1. Due to its high level of flexibility, Cruise Control is a fitness solution that is available for all persons.

2. Never go anywhere without your insulated water bottle.

3. Avoid sweeteners as much as possible.

4. Use Cruise Control-friendly sweeteners.

5. Be moderate in your use of alcohol.

SUMMARY

It is impossible to give a solution that fits all prescription for living due to the uniqueness of each individual. That is why I have designed Cruise Control to be a plan that you can do anywhere and anytime. It is important to learn and understand how to Cruise Control on the go, what to order if you are out to eat with family or friends, and which supplements and super foods will improve the quality of your life and appearance. Cruise Control is flexible enough to fit in to your desires, wants, likes, and dislikes. You will not have moments where you are on the road and oops! You forgot to bring food along, or you don't know what to order at a restaurant. Cruise Control is designed to shift gears in line with whatever is going on in your life.

Nutrition

When you have time, or remember to pack some things in your lunch sack, some great options that you might want to consider include:

bacon wrapped in paper towel,

flax crackers,

macadamia,

packets of almond or coconut butter,

fresh berries with whipped coconut milk,

celery sticks with almond butter,

Himalayan pink salt and avocado, c

cheese crisps or parm crisps,

pork rinds, s

seaweed chips... etc.

It is easy to snack in the Cruise Control way, most of my favorites require no cooking, they are:

beef jerky,

grass-fed whipped creams with berries,

pork rinds,

raw almonds,

walnuts or macadamia nuts,

tea with grass-fed butter and coconut oil,

hard-boiled eggs,

chia seed pudding,

and sunflower or pumpkin seeds.

What if you find yourself in a place without a kitchen? You might want to go for:

nuts,

nut butters,

olive oil,

MCT oil or avocado oil for vegetables and salads,

avocado,

and a snack pack of olives to add to snacks or meals.

Eating Out on Cruise Control
Since I travel a lot and frequently have business dinners and lunches, it implies that I might be eating in restaurants for days at a time. That explains why I have designed Cruise Control in such a way that it is friendly to those who frequently take dinners out. No matter where you are, you won't have trouble ordering a meal that is Cruise Control-friendly. Below are some of the dining tips:

- It is easier to make substitutions in fancy restaurants
- Check for grass-fed and gluten-free meat and dairy options
- Carry coconut oil, MCT oil, and extra virgin olive oil with you and make your own dressing
- Request beverages like unsweetened hot teas, coffee and sparkling or filtered water

Smart Food Shopping

While at the grocery store, my favorite tips for saving money are:

(1) don't just stay on the perimeter

(2) grab on-sale meat

(3) buy coconut oil

(4) stick to lower-cost seeds and nuts

(5) plan on eating similar foods

(6) avoid pre-packaged foods

(7) don't be distracted by new food items, and

(8) eat seasonally.

Cruise Control-friendly Sweeteners

Try as much as possible to avoid all sweeteners, and that is because your taste bud is designed to adapt to the food you feed them with. That implies that if you consistently take meals without sweeteners, you will soon start to enjoy those meals. Plus, since you have been eating the Cruise Control way, you will notice that you know longer crave sugar the way you used to. Alright, I know you are going to want to have a treat from time to time, so some Cruise Control-friendly sugars are:

monk fruit,

stevia,

xylitol.

You can find them in most health food stores.

Navigating Roadblocks

Life, as we know it, comes with a lot of road blocks, and Cruise Control in not an exception. A major road block for a lot of persons is lack of sleep. Some of the tips for sleeping better are:

(1) create a sanctuary

(2) give your bed a makeover

(3) add a chill effect

(4) shower before you sleep

(5) have a nightly massage

(6) have a set bedtime

(7) have a night-time tea, and

(8) track your snooze time.

CHAPTER 10: YOU'VE GOT QUESTIONS, I'VE GOT ANSWERS

KEY TAKEAWAYS

1. You burn fat when you fast, not muscles.

2. It is possible to be a vegan on Cruise Control.

3. Close monitoring is needed for diabetics on Cruise Control.

4. You can take your usual vitamins and supplements during the Burn Zone.

5. There is no room for nutrient deficiency on Cruise Control.

SUMMARY

I have taught my Cruise Control diet to several clients and online Cruisers over the years, and I must say that I have had to answer a whole lot of questions about it. This chapter provides concise answers to the most common questions that I have had to provide answers to.

Here are some of the questions that they have asked about fasting, and my answer to those questions:

Won't My Body Slip into Starvation Mode When I Fast?

Starvation is not something that gets to happen in sixteen hours, not even in several days. In order to go into starvation mode, you would have severely reduced access to food for months. It is true that each time you restrict calories, you put your body in a form of "starvation mode", but this is not a type of calorie debt that is dangerous to your body. The simple truth is that the problem for the vast majority of us today is not starvation – it is that we are chronically being overfed.

Will Fasting Burn Up My Muscle Tissue?

Fat is what you burn when you fast, not muscle. Your body is a highly intelligent machine that is engineered biologically to survive periods of food scarcity. A major reason why our body stores fat is so that it is available when food is scarce. Our muscle is made of much more complex proteins that are not easily accessible to your body. Only in extreme circumstances, when your overall body fat drops below 4 per cent, will your body begin to feed on muscle.

Will I Get Low Blood Sugar When I Fast?

One of the first thing that people do when they begin to feel shaky or dizzy is to take orange juice or honey because they assume that it must be that their blood sugar is low. That is not how blood sugar works though! Remember that insulin keeps a constant watch on your blood sugar. During the time of the day that you are not eating, your body breaks down glycogen. This happens every night while you sleep.

Doesn't fasting slow down my metabolism?
The first thing that you need to know is that Cruise Control isn't fasting, and if it was, it wouldn't shut down your metabolism. Rather, it would accelerate it! You are designed to increase your metabolic functions when your insulin is low, and it will be very low during your burn zone.

Will I Become Nutrient-Deficient?
During the Cruise Control Boost Zone, you will provide your body with meals that are packed with nutrients. These meals will contain all the minerals, vitamins, carbs, fats, and proteins your body could want. Simply put, on Cruise Control, there is simply no time for nutrient deficiency.

CRUISING FAQS

Can I Eat as Frequently as I Want During the Cruise Zone?
Yes! You can eat whatever, and whenever you feel like during your boost window. It takes your tummy about 20 minutes to register food, so take your time to know when you are satisfied.

What about Coffee, Tea, Cream, Or Milk During the Burn Zone?

Yes, I encourage that you take coffee and tea since they are appetite suppressants. Cream and milk? Not so good, but you will be ok if you add just a little.

Isn't Breakfast the Key to Weight Loss? How Then Can Skipping It Be Healthy?

Please not that you won't be skipping breakfast, you can always enjoy coffee or tea. Also, recent research also shows that skipping breakfast reduces the number of calories a person eats a day. Also, remember that you are free to schedule your boost and burn zones at any time that is convenient for you.

ONWARD! THE OPEN ROAD: WEEK FIVE AND BEYOND

KEY TAKEAWAYS

1. Now that you have arrived at your final destination, your next objective is to never quit, but to keep living all the lessons you have learnt from the Cruise Control program.

2. Cruise Control is not a diet or a fad or a temporary thingy. It is a lifestyle.

3. In order to consolidate your gains by continuing to live the Cruise Control lifestyle, you can let me be your online coach. Check out my Platinum Program at JorgeCruise.com.

4. Or you can let this book coach you by revisiting this book frequently and following the guidelines and menus all over again.

5. Or you can be your own coach. The required guidelines, tips, strategies, knowledge, food lists, meals, recipes, and meal planners, etc. have all been provided to you via this book. So just take over! Take control! Take charge! Coach yourself. You can do it!

6. Stay in touch with the Cruise Control program at JorgeCruise.com.; Facebook.com/JorgeCruise; and #CruiseControlDiet.

SUMMARY

Congratulations are in order now that you have arrived at your final destination. So, what next? Where do you go from here?

Well, your next journey or objective awaits you! And that is to never quit, but instead to keep living all the lessons you have learnt from the Cruise Control program. Remember that Cruise Control is not a diet or a fad or a momentary, temporary affair. Cruise Control is, indeed, a lifestyle! It's a way you should live your life for optimal health, fitness and longevity. Cruise Control can trigger long-lasting positive changes in your life. But to get there, you also require a long-term, lifetime commitment to the program.

YOUR CHOICES

So, what next? Where do you go from here? Well, here, I give you some good ideas of how you could keep consolidating your gains by continuing to live the Cruise Control lifestyle. Here are the options:

1. Let Me Be Your Coach: I can coach you. I have an online program (the Platinum program) under which I can coach you and provide you with new meal planners, meals, menus and recipes that are all complaint with the Cruise Control requirements. This way you are relieved of the stress of managing your weight control effort. Check out my Platinum program at JorgeCruise.com.

2. Let the Book Coach You: You can also let the book coach you by simply going back to the first 4 weeks and just following the guidelines and menu all over again. You can never get bored as there are so many delicious recipes in the book. Have loads of fun!

3. Be Your Own Coach (BYOC): You can also be the coach. Yes, you! At this point you should be able to now coach yourself. All the relevant and required knowledge has been imparted in you via this book. Food lists, meals, recipes, meal planners have all been provided to you. Now you should be able to comfortably ensconce yourself into the driver's seat of your health, fitness and weight control lifestyle. Now you can create your own menus, reorder meal plans, switch and swap meals and snacks. You can take control. Yes, you can take Cruise Control. Cruise Control is a health, fitness and weight-loss lifestyle that helps you to live your best healthiest life ever!

You can do it!

JorgeCruise.com
Facebook.com/JorgeCruise

#CruiseControlDiet

Hey! Be assured. Cruise Control is just so much fun and you'll see as soon as you get started.

So, here's to a healthier, slimmer, more good-looking, happier, prosperous you!

Cheers!

Now, let's go!

APPENDIX A: THE GROUNDBREAKING SCIENCE BEHIND CRUISE CONTROL

KEY TAKEAWAYS

1. The pattern of eating on Cruise Control boosts your Mitochondria, which then improves your level of insulin sensitivity.

2. Cruise Control will help your body build needed antioxidants and burn free radicals.

3. Cruise Control directly burns belly fat.

4. The pattern of eating on Cruise Control will reduce your risk of heart disease, cancer, and diabetes.

5. Following the Cruise Control program will improve your memory, focus, and clarity. You will also reduce anxiety, stress, depression.

6. Cruise Control takes advantage of the regenerative and natural healing processes in your brain and body and ensures that you live better and longer (increases longevity).

SUMMARY

The power of Cruise Control cannot be overemphasized. I have seen first-hand, tremendous transformation in my clients. The level of success seen in my clients is due to the simple fact that I have built on my past recommendations for moving and eating in a way that shows honor for the human biological design.

Not only will you rid your body of excess weight, you will also build lean and sleek muscles. You will sleep better at night and have more energy each day. Let me be clear on this: this is not another restrictive diet; neither is it a complicated regimen. It is simply a fantastic design for living that is supported by substantial evidence.

Power Up Your Mitochondria

Inside our cells, there are mini organs known as Mitochondria. They are responsible for several functions that keeps the body healthy, strong, and young, including promoting the growth of new cells and regulating the cells' energy flow. This is how you prevent aging! The pattern of eating on Cruise Control boosts your Mitochondria, which then improves your level of insulin sensitivity.

Giving Adequate Time for Cleaning and Repairing

Cruise Control will help your body build needed antioxidants and burn free radicals. It does this by giving your body the needed downtime to clean up waste, do repairs, and take out the trash.

Burn Off Belly Fat Like You've Never Done Before

Taking myself as a case study, I have seen that Cruise Control directly burns belly fat. During the Burn Zone period of Cruise Control, your body has to work in order to find energy- this is a major reason why you burn fat during Burn Zone. Another reason you burn fat is that restricting your Boost Zone revs up your metabolism.

The receptors in your body are also activated by the Burn Zone. These receptors increase fat burning.

Become A Machine That Fights Diseases

Various studies have shown that eating on Cruise Control will reduce your risk of heart disease, cancer, and diabetes.

Sharpen Your Mind

Apart from all the physical promises of Cruise Control, one thing I appreciate most about Cruise Control is the fact that following a Burn/Boost zone schedule on a daily basis will improve your memory, focus, and clarity. You will also reduce anxiety, stress, depression, and have a more stable emotional balance than you've never had.

Live A Healthier, Longer Life!

Cruise Control takes advantage of the regenerative and natural healing processes in your brain and body and ensure you live better and longer. Eating on a regular Burn to Boost schedule has been shown to slow don most age-related diseases and conditions, and helps you live a healthy and happy life in later years.

One of the ways this is naturally done by your body is with the help of human growth hormone. This hormone plays a vital role in the growth of adolescents and children. It also plays an important part in the repair process that happens in your body every night when you sleep by telling some cells to divide and regenerate. The human growth hormone is all about encouraging the duplication, repair, and regeneration of your cells.

You see, the most potent way to signal growth hormone is by not eating for sixteen hours. Studies show that following the Cruise Control method will double the production of your growth hormone in just five days.

NOTES

NOTES

NOTES

RECOMMENDED FOR YOU!

V

Made in the USA
Lexington, KY
08 August 2019